Around
Lake Constance.

STADLER

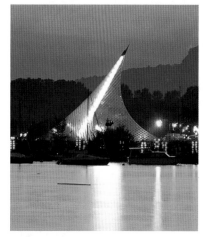

Verlag Stadler Konstanz

Constance ● ● ● ● ● ● ● ● ● ● ● ●

What would the Lake be without the metropolis of Constance? A modern city with a lively history, a university town since 1966 with a campus for some 10000 students on the outskirts. Student life can be found in the winding, medieval alleyways: pubs and wine bars galore in historic buildings around the late Gothic minster, and a host of different cultural events. Near the minster, the visitor finds a prime example of the mixture of history and modern times: just opposite the minster stands the new, bright red building of the Constance Culture Centre with a library, a gallery and ample space for various cultural activities.

Old and new also blend at the harbour: the ships of the White Fleet commence their cruises across Lake Constance at the very place where formerly cargo ships laden with furs, linen and spices used to dock. One building was of particular importance to trade in medieval Constance, and it still stands out today. Built in 1388 as a trading house, the „Konzil" building was named after the Council of Constance (1414-18), during which the only ever papal election on German soil took place in 1417. The impressive „Imperia" statue on the quay stands witness of this event; the monument created by the contemporary artist, Peter Lenk from Bodman-Ludwigshafen, has received both praise and criticism.

The harbour is the starting point of a hiking track along the Constance Funnel, leading through the municipal gardens set up in the 19th century amidst remnants of towers and gates, past the old Dominican monastery on an island which today is a hotel of the Steigenberger Group, across the old Rhine bridge, along the 19th century lake promenade „Seestrasse", to the leisure centre including the Jakobsbad and Hörnle swimming pools. Swimming in the Hörnle pool has always been free of charge, and from here, visitors can marvel at the largest fireworks on the Lake which form the highlight of the annual Constance Seenachtsfest Festival in Constance Bay in August.

A busy summer street café

6 The Konzil, a former trading hall dating back to 1388, and the harbour clock

Constance Harbour, Imperia, the Konzil (above), and quay   **7**

The Island of Reichenau

When the former abbot of the Island of Reichenau Monastery, Walahfrid Strabo, wrote the poem „de culturam hortorum" about herbs in his monk's cell between 830 and 840, he could not possibly imagine that today's vegetable gardening, together with fishing, wine growing and the cultural heritage in monasteries and churches, would bring such wealth to the population. In his book, which must have been the first gardening book in Germany, the abbot described 24 herbs and plants for cooking, medicinal and ornamental purposes, many of which are still grown today. As a little boy, Walahfrid went to school at the Reichenau Benedictine Monastery, which was founded by the travelling bishop Pirmin in 724 A. D. In those days, it was one of the most important abbeys of the Franconian Empire and remained the spiritual and cultural centre of Europe for two centuries.

The Romanesque churches of St. George, St. Mary and Mark, and St. Peter and Paul are silent witnesses of this cradle of occidental culture. In the early 9th century, the library became one of the most significant libraries of its time, and it is still famous today. During the 10th and 11th centuries, the abbey's book and mural painting school had its heyday; the abbey was dissolved in 1757. Some of the precious works of art can be found in the local heritage museum, the minster's treasury and on the church walls.

In honour of the abbot Walahfrid, the „Hortulus" monastery garden has been reconstructed. Smelling and tasting samples of the medicinal herbs are free of charge. Some 120 full-time and several dozens of part-time gardeners feel honoured when visitors watch them working like busy bees in their fields, harvesting several million lettuces, 2.5 million kohlrabis and 1.8 million radishes each year. The number one vegetable, however, is the cucumber: more than 12 million are sold throughout the country as nutritious promoter of the largest island in Lake Constance. The people of Reichenau know very well why they have to preserve their „rich pasture" on their beautiful island with its unique climate. It comes as no surprise, for in their vicinity, directly on the dam connecting the island with the mainland, lies the Wollmatinger Ried, a marshland of 1917 acres and Baden-Württemberg's largest nature reserve. Endangered plant and animal species have found a sanctuary here, such as the wagtail, various types of water fowl, the Siberian iris and the extremely rare Lake Constance forget-me-not. Such special species will be preserved here for future generations.

The Island of Reichenau and the 11th century St. Peter and Paul Church, Niederzell **9**

10   Ottonic mural paintings (above) and St. George's Church in Oberzell, built between 888 and 913

Plastic green houses (above) and an idyllic scene in Niederzell

The Reichenau quay opposite the Swiss shores

One of the last fishermen of Reichenau (above). Drying fishing nets **13**

14   The Island of Mainau (above), springtime Alpine panorama

Mainau ● ● ● ● ● ● ●

The ideal time for a walk around the island is early on a summer morning. Before the large car park fills up and the ships bring hoards of tourists across the lake, the park and the gardens are peaceful and undisturbed. The Island of Mainau is the largest tourist attraction on the Lake with approximately 1.7 million visitors per year. And yet, the island, with all its subtropical plants, seems to be a small paradise. It is famous for its rich blossoms in every season, from tulips and daffodils in early spring, to beautiful and rich rose blossoms in summer and the dahlia show in early autumn, boasting every colour of the rainbow. Owing to its Mediterranean character, the Island of Mainau has banana trees, palms and citric fruit as well as an arboretum with gigantic trees. Some of them are more than 100 years old and were planted by Grand Duke Frederic I of Baden, who founded this garden paradise on Lake Constance. In 1932, he left the island to his great grandson, Count Lennart Bernadotte, who opened it to the public and transformed the once over-grown gardens into a floral paradise. He also restored the splendid Baroque buildings on the island: the richly decorated church, built by Johann Kaspar Bagnato, and the three-winged castle which was also built by Bagnato and is now the home of the Bernadotte family.

Today, the Island of Mainau is more than just a floral paradise. The „Island of Five Seasons" offers beautiful nature and interesting culture, with travelling exhibitions at the castle, and concerts in the castle grounds on mild summer nights. Not only do visitors come in good weather, for even on rainy days or during the autumn and winter months, there are many interesting attractions, e. g. a multivision show in the garden tower, or the butterfly house which is open all the year round and where visitors can observe a multitude of butterflies from European, tropical and subtropical regions at close range. The new palm house protects the exotic plants during cold winters and offers many special attractions between autumn and spring.

The Baroque St. Mary's Castle Church on Mainau and the Italian rose garden   **15**

Bodanrück is the name of the promontory between Lake Überlingen and the Lower Lake, and it is still considered to be a special secret among insiders. Far away from the major trunk roads, forests, fields and meadows offer peace and relaxation. An extensive network of hiking tracks invites the visitor to walk or cycle along the promontory and marvel at the view down below. Every now and then, the tracks lead to small, tidy villages with cosy pubs and restaurants. Several castles, sometimes hidden from view, round up this idyllic picture. Freudental Castle, for example, is a beautiful Baroque building dating back to 1699, with splendid stucco ceilings and paintings. Another manor-type castle worth seeing is Langenrain Castle which was built at the end of the 17th century.

From Langenrain, a hiking track leads to the medieval castle ruins of Kargegg some one-and-a-half miles to the northeast. The track then descends to Lake Überlingen and the legendary Maria Gorge, a ravine with a length of some 110 yards and, at places, a width of only one yard, with rock walls of up to 70 yards in height. On the banks of the Lake, when the water level is low, you may be able to see the Devil's Table, a rock plateau attracting many divers, some of which unfortunately never returned to the surface alive.

The Allensbach leisure and deer park on Bodanrück is much appreciated by families. Covering an area of 185 acres, local animals that are hardly found in nature today, such as brown bears, lynxes and wolves have found a home in large enclosures. Lake Mindelsee is in close proximity to the leisure park. It is a moraine lake dating back to the ice age, and it is said to have an underground connection to Lake Constance. The small lake has a certain magic, and its shores are a precious biotope of rich vegetation under preservation order. At some places, swimming is allowed. Mindelsee is covered by water lilies, and the rare catfish is still at home here, as are many types of water fowl.

Lake Mindelsee near Möggingen, an idyllic nature reserve on the Bodanrück 17

Picturesque Freudental Castle, built between 1698 and 1700

Allensbach on Lake Gnadensee, with the Island of Reichenau in the background 19

Radolfzell ● ● ● ● ● ● ● ● ●

At nine o'clock on a Saturday morning, the scent of freshly cut flowers, of vegetables harvested the previous evening, and of fresh fish from the Lower Lake lies over the Market Square in Radolfzell. Farmers from the Höri Peninsula opposite Radolfzell and from Bodanrück offer a colourful display of their produce between the beautiful minster of „Our Blessed Lady", the Austrian castle and the beautifully renovated burgher houses. After a shopping spree on the market, people go to have a pre-lunch drink in the old part of town, either at Weinstube Baum, at „Scharfe Eck" or at Münsterstüble where guests enjoy a glass of wine with the locals who sometimes reveal a secret on how to spend a very special day on the Lake.

Seestrasse is a prime example of the picturesque town centre. Old 18th century fishermen's and farmer's houses with their enormous barn doors and gabled roofs stand witness of times gone by. And the pillared basilica, the Minster, towers high above the town. In 826 A. D., bishop Ratoldus of Verona founded the „Cella Ratoldi" on this very spot, which was to be the foundation stone of today's metropolis on the Lake. As a capital of nature and environmental protection, Radolfzell has celebrated its efforts to create a healthy environment. The town has re-naturalized the banks of the lake by creating a shallow water zone.

The climate in these parts must be healthy, for every year, thousands of birds come to the nature reserve of the Mettnau Peninsula next to the spa where „healing by moving" has been a motto since 1958. The famous poet and painter, Joseph Victor von Scheffel, relaxed here; his castle has been well-preserved.

A visit to one of the traditional events on the Lower Lake is an absolute must: on the third Monday in July, the so-called „Hausherrenmontag", the neighbours from the Höri village of Moos sail across early in the morning in their beautifully decorated boats and are received on the banks of the lake in Radolfzell by dignitaries from church and town. This water procession dates back to a promise given some 170 years ago by the people of Moos after they had been spared from a serious cattle disease. According to the locals, God, at the end of his creation, allegedly said „Jetzt hör i auf" which means „Now I'll stop". The Höri Peninsula, with its attractive cultural highlights, innumerable orchards, and picturesque sights, has long been a sanctuary for poets and artists.

Radolzell – view from the Minster tower (above), and the lakeside promenade with the „Concert Shell"   21

Lover's Island near the Mettnau Peninsula (above), and the Mettnau Reed nature reserve

St. Blasius Chapel in Kattenhorn/Höri dates back to the 15th century 23

Trees in flower near Gaienhofen/Höri Peninsula

Fruit ● ● ● ● ● ● ● ● ● ● ●

For many centuries, orchards have enhanced the land-scape of Lake Constance. In spring, the fertile regions and valleys around the Lake are covered in a floral veil of pink and white, and in autumn, a colourful display of apples and green leaves truly catches the eye. Fruit-growing is still very important: The German side of Lake Constance counts some 2000 growers – 40 of them are organic farmers, who primarily grow apples. The German banks of the lake are considered to be the largest apple growing region in Germany. Small amounts of pears, cherries and damsons are also grown. Fruit-growers have to follow strict integrated production rules with very litt-le fertilizing and largely without using pesticides which means that apples from Lake Constance stand for quality throughout the land.

Fruit from Lake Constance can be found everywhere: during the harvest, people can either pick fruit themsel-ves or buy the produce at farms and roadside stands, on local markets and in supermarkets. A new marketing concept for regional agricultural products has been developed: special farmer's markets offer produce in Radolfzell and Constance. These markets were created to promote agriculture and preserve the old cultural land-scape for the decades to come. The concept includes the preservation of the impressive high fruit trees which, in recent decades, have often had to make way for smaller and more lucrative trees. Numerous efforts are made to preserve the orchard landscape with the produce marke-ted as juice or cider.

More information about fruit from Lake Constance can be obtained in an entertaining manner by taking a walk through the orchards, for example on „Apfelweg" (apple track) near Immenstaad-Kippenhausen, where twenty illustrated panels provide details on fruit and growing methods.

　View of the Lower Lake from the Arenenberg Castle terrace

French Empire-style room at Arenenberg Castle; the wallpaper reminds of the Napoleonic Wars   **27**

The former St. Georgen Monastery in Stein am Rhein now houses the local museum

Stein am Rhein and the Island of Werd

The Höri Peninsula is one of the most beautiful gateways to Switzerland. The Untersee, i. e. the „Lower Lake" narrows to form the Hochrhein only three kilometres from the picturesque town of Öhningen and its Augustine canonical foundation which dates back to 965 A. D. Stein owes its existence and its wealth to this transition. Even in the Middle Ages, products from „Ledisegler" freight ships had to be reloaded to the Rhine ferries at this point.

A footbridge offers access to one of the last places of paradise – the small Island of Werd in the middle of the river Rhine. Following the settlement by lake dwellers, Celts and Helvetians, the Romans used this island as bridge pier across the Rhine in 50 A. D. Today, a small two-storey gabled building is home to seven brethren of a society who live according to the rules of St. Francis. Among the reeds of this little island which is smaller than a football field, they lead a life of peaceful contemplation, celibacy and obedience, surrounded by seagulls, ducks and swans, and their own vegetable gardens. They go out from their little paradise into some communities to perform social and spiritual duties. Visitors are always welcome to attend mass in the 9th century chapel, named after St. Othmar, the first abbot of the St. Gallen Monastery. Othmar died in exile on the Island of Werd.

Stein boasts some splendid town gates, small winding alleys, impressive burgher houses and facades enhanced with frescos and oriels which are better preserved than anywhere else in Switzerland. That is why Stein is often referred to as „Rothenburg on Lake Constance". The house „Zum Weißen Adler" (White Eagle House), with its beautiful mural paintings is still owned by the Kleeblatt (shamrock) guild and is said to be one of the most beautiful buildings in Switzerland. The former Benedictine St. George Monastery on the banks of the Rhine dates back to the year 1005, but the buildings that can be visited today were built between 14th and 16th centuries. With some 30 pubs and restaurants, the medieval town offers ample opportunity to relax and sample some of the delicious Swiss delicacies such as „Röschti & Gschnetzeltes".

Towering high above the town, the 12th century Hohenklingen Castle offers a splendid view across the Rhine and the surrounding area. West of Stein and halfway to Schaffhausen, the small town of Diessenhofen is well worth a visit. An old wooden bridge connects this medieval town with the German community of Gailingen. 180 years ago, soldiers marched to war against Napoleon across this all-enclosed bridge.

Splendid fresco paintings in Stein am Rhein (above), and the Island of Werd with the pilgrimage chapel of St. Othmar

View of Schaffhausen and the striking 16th century Munot Fortress

Romantic scene in the Hegau region

The interesting volcanic Hegau region (above), and the Hohentwiel Castle Ruins   33

● ● ● ● ● ● ● Bodman, Sipplingen

A typical scene on Lake Constance: beautiful weather, cotton-wool clouds and sunshine which – depending on the time of day – displays the lake in many different shades of green and blue. Stormy winds and gentle breezes invite people to go sailing, swimming or enjoy outings in their motor boats. Covering an area of 355 square miles, the lake is home to some 55300 registered water vehicles ranging from steam, motor and pedal boats to 13-yard yachts and the giants of the White Fleet. There is something only few people are aware of: Lake Constance serves as drinking water reservoir for 4.5 million people, with nine German and eight Swiss waterworks processing some 220 million cubic yards of the precious liquid per annum.

Near Sipplingen, BWV (Lake Constance Waterworks) on the northern banks of the lake takes 470000 cubic yards of drinking water per day from a depth of 197 feet and 40 feet above the lake bottom. This water is also available in bottles as „Lake Constance Crystal Table Water". BWV is entitled to take as much as 875,000 cubic yards, or 177 million gallons. 1066 gallons of water are pumped per second. The state-of-the-art waterworks 340 yards above the picturesque former wine-growing villa-ge of Sipplingen is open to visitors at all times. Once the precious liquid is processed, the water is pumped via 995 miles of pipeline into various regions in Baden-Württemberg, supplying approximately 3.6 million people in 173 communities.

The part of the lake referred to as Lake Überlingen ends a few miles away from Sipplingen near the communities of Bodman and Ludwigshafen. The villages are divided by a beautiful nature reserve. Good walkers should climb up and visit the 17th century Frauenberg convent with its pilgrimage chapel and visitor's terrace, or go on a hiking tour to the Alt-Bodman castle ruins.

One of the most splendid hiking trails along the lake starts at the castle of the Counts of Bodman and end at Maria Gorge. The village itself is one of the oldest settlements on the Lake, and the 8th century imperial palace is said to have given Lacus Bodamicus, or Lake Bodman its name.

View of Überlingen (above), and the quay

Salem Castle, re-built between 1596 and 1600 after a great fire

Salem-Unteruhldingen ● ● ● ● ●

Built in 1750, the pilgrimage church of Birnau on the northern shore of Lake Constance towers high above the water, fields and vineyards as if it was made to protect the entire region from evil. Behind the church, the traffic passes by on a major trunk road, but in front of it, visitors can marvel at the entire splendour of the lake, the Bodanrück mountain range and the Island of Mainau. Just down below lies Kloster Maurach, a former convent which now serves as convention centre. Birnau was built by architect Peter Thumb and the interior designer Joseph Anton Feuchtmayer. It is a prime example of Baroque architecture: splendid paintings, stucco ceilings and angels such as the famous „honey licker".

Only a few miles away, the tourist village of Uhldingen-Mühlhofen, known for its environmental protection campaigns and traffic-free village centre, offers a very special highlight: houses on stilts. For the last 75 years, the world-famous lake dwelling museum has attracted visitors from all over the world. 15 houses stand on some 2000 posts just above the lake, giving an idea the everyday life of the people who used to live here in the Stone and Bronze Ages some 5000 years ago. Even today, archaeologists still find remnants on the shores or on diving expeditions in the winter months.

Seefelden is situated between Unteruhldingen and Birnau. This small, most beautiful hamlet, with its romantic setting directly on the lake, is one of the region's oldest parishes and a popular destination on Sunday afternoon walks along the shores of the lake through the Seefelder Aach nature reserve.

A few miles further inland near the 50-acre Affenberg monkey park lies Salem Castle, surrounded by rolling hills and beautiful ponds. The name is famous: in 1920, Chancellor Prince Max von Baden and the politician and teacher, Kurt Hahn, founded the well-known Salem boarding school. The impressive old walls cover an area of 42 acres and were built as a Cistercian monastery in 1137. Owned by the Margrave of Baden since 1804, the castle offers some interesting samples of occidental culture, ranging from travelling exhibitions, to a firebrigade museum, a craft centre, a cooper's museum and the margravial wine cellars. „New life in the old castle" is the motto. The most interesting building within this complex, however, is the Gothic 14th century minster, a stone witness of half a millenium.

One of the Salem Castle gates (above). Reconstruction of an early Stone-Age village on stilts in Uhldingen

Famous work of art of J.A. Feuchtmayer (1696-1770): the pilgrimage church of Birnau, its „honey licker" and interior

Surrounded by vineyards lies Birnau, offering a view of the Upper Lake and the Alps

The Old Castle in Meersburg dates back to 628. It is one of the oldest inhabited castles in Germany

A view of Meersburg from the Lake (above), and view of the New Castle built in 1750   **43**

The wine-growing village of Hagnau and Mount Säntis in the background

The wine ● ● ● ● ● ● ● ● ● ● ●

Even the ancient Romans were familiar with the heat accumulation effect of Lake Constance on wine growing: the legions of Tiberius allegedly brought the first vines from the sunny south. In later years it was the monks who continued the wine-growing tradition. Under abbot Haito I, the first vine was planted on the Island of Reichenau, and a few decades later, the clergyman and scholar, Walahfrid Strabo, called 40 vintners from Steckborn (on the Swiss shore) to the island to expand the winegrowing which remained the centre of agriculture for many centuries to follow. There were times when winegrowing covered 495 acres. In 1896, the Reichenau Winegrowers' Cooperative was founded. Today, the vineyards only cover 37 acres of land, producing some splendid Müller-Thurgau, Blauburgunder, Grauburgunder, Kerner and Gutedel wines which go extremely well with fish. However, you must be very quick if you are hoping to keep some of these rare wines in you cellar, because most of the bottles are only sold on the island itself. After all, the people of Reichenau know about hospitality and the best wines for their guests. Wines from Kressbronn, Ermatingen, Konstanz, Mount Hohentwiel in the Hegau region and from Gailingen on the Rhine are just as popular.

The first Baden winegrowers' cooperative was founded on 20th October 1881 in Hagnau on the lake by the clergyman and writer, Dr. Heinrich Hansjakob. Today, the cooperative counts 130 members within 60 winegrowing families who grow their grapes on an area of 320 acres. They produce 1.2 million litres of „Sonnenufer" and „Burgstall" wine from Hagnau per annum. Situated on the northern banks of the lake, the village of Hagnau only has moderate average temperatures, but the heat accumulating effect of Lake Constance ensures very balanced temperatures throughout the year. In autumn, there is much sunshine and a clear sky, and at an altitude of 1300 to 1450 feet the fertile moraine soil around Hagnau is the ideal location to grow the Hagnau Müller-Thurgau wine which is considered to be one of the finest whine wines in Baden. In 1884, a winegrowers' cooperative was founded in the neighbouring town of Meersburg. Today, several full and part-time winegrowers grow their produce on 123 acres of land. One of the very special rarities is the Trockenbeerenauslese with 165 degrees Oechsle. The Meersburg winegrowers and the State Winery grow their grapes on the steep slopes of Meersburg and in Stetten, but they are also masters of quite a different trade: with ingredients such as yeast, apples, cherries and pears they produce a very fine liquor which brings back memories of the lake and the landscape long after your holidays.

Hagnau Church during the fruit blossom 45

46   The Zeppelin Museum in Friedrichshafen (above), and the lakeside promenade

Friedrichshafen

Friedrichshafen in brief: Zeppelins and aviation, museums, high tech and automotive industry, ZF, MTU and the Zeppelin Metallwerke, conventions and conferences and, of course, the trade fair centre with twelve to sixteen international exhibitions per year, e.g. Interboot, Eurobike and AERO, the aviation fair. People meet in Friedrichshafen, or „FN", to enjoy an ice-cream or cappucino on the lakeside promenade, to participate in cultural programmes at Fischbach Station, or to get a kick out of rock music at the former Fallenbrunnen barracks. An increasing number of major events with international orchestras and rock and pop stars are staged at the enormous halls of the trade fair centre and at Graf Zeppelin House, Friedrichshafen's number one address next to the yacht harbour at the end of the lakeside promenade. It boasts three large halls, ten conference rooms, a restaurant and a café.

It was the great builder of airships, Count Ferdinand von Zeppelin, who brought lasting fame and fortune to the Swabian Lake Constance metropolis at the beginning of the 20th century. The first of his legendary „flying cigars" took off at Friedrichshafen-Manzell on 2nd July 1900 to conquer the world. Even today, almost a hundred years later, the locally developed and newly built Zeppelin NT (Zeppelin of New Technologies) appears in the sky and may go down in history like its predecessors. Once again, people stand still and marvel at this grand sight. The new Zeppelin has its own gigantic hangar, one of the largest halls in Southern Germany which was specially built for it near Löwental Airport.

The splendid old harbour station is now home to the Zeppelin Museum Friedrichshafen – a museum of technology and art, where visitors can follow the maiden voyage of LZ 127 Graf Zeppelin from Lakehurst via Friedrichshafen, Tokyo, Los Angeles and back to Lakehurst in 1929. Inside the striking Bauhaus building there is a 44-yard reconstruction of part of the 268-yard LZ 129 „Hindenburg" zeppelin – built according to the original plans and with the original tools - including some sparsely furnished cabins and light aluminium beds and the noble salon. Old documentation, modern computer terminals and industrial products present aviation history and Count Zeppelin's heritage. The 37670 square feet exhibition space also houses works of art from five centuries, with paintings and sculptures from the Middle Ages to the present day. Only a few yards away on the lakefront stands the School Museum which was faithfully reconstructed down to the most minor detail. The old classrooms show how little „good-for-nothings" used to feel the cane. Collections of Norbert Steinhauser, a former school principal from Friedrichshafen, and of professor Erich Müller from Weingarten are on display, with numerous fascinating items such as old inkpots, nib boxes, pictures, maps and, of course, zeppelins.

Montfort Castle in Langenargen, built in the Moorish style in the 19th century

The quay in Langenargen (above). Idyllic scene on the terrace of the Montfort Castle café 51

St. George's Castle (1585) on the Wasserburg Peninsula, a former church complex of the St. Gallen Monastery

Wasserburg ● ● ● ● ● ● ●

The Wasserburg skyline must be one of the most photographed motifs on Lake Constance. The idyllic peninsula on the Bavarian shores catches the eye even from afar. The castle, with its picturesque gable, the onion-shaped tower of St. George's Church, the Malhaus and Fuggerhaus blend in to form one picturesque entity, and the small bay has therefore often been referred to as „painter's corner". Until 1720, the peninsula was an island, and it boasts a unique history: it was first mentioned as a dominion of the St. Gallen Monastery in 784; during the 10th century, it served as refuge against the Huns; it then became the property of the Counts of Montfort who sold Wasserburg to the Augsburg merchant family Fugger in the 16th century. The Fuggers remained masters on the island until 1755, and it was also the Fuggers who filled the water ditch between the island and the mainland, thus creating a peninsula in 1720. The Fugger Column, with relief decorations at the entrance to the peninsula, commemorates this event. Wasserburg belonged to Austria for 50 years and changed hands to the Bavarians in 1805.

The history of the buildings is as varied as the island's history. St. George's Church, in its present shape and its classicistic interior, was built in the early 19th century after a late Gothic building and the Baroque church had been severely damaged by a fire in the 17th century. The castle dates back to the 13th century and stands on the remains of a Roman military outpost. Over the years, there have been numerous alterations and additions. Since 1812, the castle has been private property and today serves as a hotel. The local museum provides details of the history. It is located in the Malhaus which was built by the Fuggers as court house in the 16th century.

The cemetery with its defensive wall on the lakeside is well worth a visit. Horst Wolfram Geissler, the author of the novel „Der liebe Augustin" published in 1921, has found his last place of rest here. Some of his novel plays in Wasserburg. The famous author Martin Walser was born in Wasserburg in 1927 and today lives in Nussdorf near Überlingen.

54   The start of the great Lake Constance Regatta „Around Lake Constance" (above). Surfing near Langenargen

Canoeing on the Lower Lake, and the last of the Lake Constance paddle steamers: „Hohentwiel"

Lindau Harbour at dawn

Lindau ● ● ● ● ● ● ● ● ● ● ●

Lindau exudes an almost Mediterranean atmosphere which is omnipresent in its cafés, on the waterfront promenade with its magnificent view of the lighthouse and the Bavarian lion, in its romantic alleys and in the suburbs with their splendid villas and manor houses. The geniune Lindauer, however, resides on the Bavarian island and enjoys the panoramic view of Lake Constance and the Alps.

Since 1976, the island's historic buildings and monuments have been under protection. The island itself only covers 148 acres. Visitors can easily walk the 655 yards from the northern to the southern shore, and all the sights are no more than 10 minutes away, provided one does not spend too much time in the winding alleys or in the famous Maximilianstrasse with its cobblestones that date back a thousand years. Lindau is a paradise for hobby photographers, and the warm welcome in numerous wine bars, inns, shops and boutiques even attracts people from Milan to cross the Alps and go on a spree in „Little Venice".

The most famous sight is the harbour with its old 13th century lighthouse; the new 110 feet lighthouse and the Bavarian lion (built in the mid-19th century) mark the entrance to the harbour. A visit to the old Town Hall, built in 1422 and renovated in 1975 according to plans dating back to 1885, and to the municipal theatre – which used to be a church – is an absolute must. The landscape of the Bavarian shores is dominated by orchards, and on Wednesday and Saturday mornings, farmers offer their produce on the market square between the protestant church of St. Stephan and the catholic church of the former convent. Directly opposite the church stands the Baroque „Haus zum Cavazzen" which is said to be the „most beautiful burgher house on Lake Constance". It was rebuilt after a great fire in 1729 and boasts some magnificent mural paintings. Since 1929 it has served as City Museum and houses an impressive collection of mechanical music instruments. The „Diebs- und Malefizturm" (Thieves' Tower) and the 1000-year-old St. Peter's church, one of the oldest buildings in this region, can be found on Schrannenplatz square. And just around the corner you can find the Goldenes Lamm Inn which partly dates back to the 15th century and offers some delicious Bavarian white sausage and a cool Salvator beer in its cosy Alte Stube. Make sure you get there in time, for the famous Bavarian white sausage must traditionally be consumed before the clock strikes twelve (midday).

58   The famous Lindau landmarks: the Bavarian Lion and the Old Town Hall (above), and Maximilianstrasse

Lindau Harbour and the famous Bavarion Lion

64   View of Bregenz and the lakeside stage, the extremely popular venue of the Bregenz Festival

● ● ● ● ● Bregenz/Pfänder/KUB

Bregenz, on the eastern end of Lake Constance, is the regional and cultural capital of the Austrian state of Vorarlberg. The best way to start exploring Bregenz is a trip to Mount Pfänder (3359 ft) towering high above the city. Only a stone's throw away from the city centre, the funicular terminal takes visitors up in spacious panoramic cabins all the year round. At the top, a breathtaking view awaits the visitor: the entire Bregenz Bay of Lake Constance stretches out like an enormous amphitheatre.

Numerous hiking and cycling tracks lead across to the German Allgäu, or down to the Lake. The 5-mile „Käsewanderweg" (cheese track), for example, invites the hiker to find out more about cheese-making at alpine dairy farms, or sample some special delicacies at one of the alpine inns and pubs. In winter, the region is a skiing and tobogganing paradise.

The Mount Pfänder funicular top terminal also marks the gateway to the Alpine Deer Park where ibeces, red deer stags, wild boars and marmots live in peace. Admission is free, and between spring and autumn, falconers present white-headed and golden eagles, falcons and mountain vultures and provide background information on these endangered species.

Life pulsates in the city down below which offers an enormous cultural range throughout the year. Vorarlberg, the smallest Austrian state, boasts some 1000 cultural events per annum. Some have reached inter national fame, such as the Bregenz Festival and the Schubertiade. In July and August, the stage on the lake attracts many visitors. In 1946, the stage was nothing but an old barge, but today, the stage setting is rebuilt every two years on several hundred posts in the lake. The Festival House next to the outdoor stage is, no doubt, a sight well worth visiting.

The Bregenz House of Art „Kunsthaus Bregenz", or KUB, in the town centre is one of the architectural highlights in Vorarlberg. The striking, and yet discreet, glass building is of particular beauty at night. Travelling exhibitions can be found inside. The medieval old part of town with its picturesque timber-framed houses lies a little further away. Deuring Castle in the old town has been open to the public since the 17th century. It is run by the Huber family who are famous for their Austrian delicacies. The people of Bregenz are very proud of the „Old Rhine" nature reserve and the Rhine delta with its beautiful hiking tracks.

The Pfänder Deer Park (above). Fun and leisure in Vorarlberg **67**

View of the Upper Lake, the Island of Lindau and Constance from Mount Pfänder

Obersee, the „Upper Lake" ● ● ● ● ●

Lake Constance is often referred to as the „Lake between three countries". This primarily applies to the Upper Lake, surrounded by the German states of Baden-Württemberg and Bavaria, the Austrian state of Vorarlberg, and the Swiss cantons of St. Gallen and Thurgau. No-one has ever tried to define which part of the lake belonged to whom, and there is no international agreement on national territories. Only for the Constance Funnel, as it is called, and for the Lower Lake, an agreement dating back to the mid-19th century applies, where the border between Germany and Switzerland is said to be approximately in the middle.

Constance and Bregenz, two historic towns, mark the two poles of the Upper Lake at opposite ends of the longest stretch of 28.6 miles. One of the White Fleet ships regularly sails this distance in approximately four hours. Half-way, between Fischbach near Friedrichshafen and the Swiss town of Uttwil, the Lake has its deepest spot with 827 feet; the widest stretch lies between Kressbronn and Rorschach, where the German shore is about 9 miles away from the Swiss shore. There is no fixed connection across the lake, but there are two „sailing links": the ferries between Constance-Staad and Meersburg, and between Friedrichshafen and Romanshorn. Not only do they transport cars, passengers and pedestrians all the year round, but also lorries and an increasing number of bicycles. During the summer season, the Lake is home to thousands of sailing and motor boats as well as regular and excursion liners which stop at every major village. The absolute star on the water is the historic paddle steamer „Hohentwiel": every little detail of the original steamer was reconstructed. The „Hohentwiel" was inaugurated in 1990 and is used as excursion liner through the summer.

When the winter temperatures reach extremely low levels, the Lake freezes over completely and all wheels stand still. This so-called „Seegförne" is an event that only happens once in a century on Lake Constance, with the most recent one in 1963 which was celebrated by the population for several weeks.

The Rohrspitz nature reserve on the Rhine Delta between Austria and Switzerland

Mount Säntis ● ● ● ● ● ● ● ●

Whenever the Föhn wind blows it looks as if it was rising up from the Lake itself; every minute detail is visible, and it seems to be dominating the impressive Alpine panorama: Mount Säntis, with an altitude of 8,207 feet the highest mountain of the Alpstein range in eastern Switzerland, is referred to as „The Mountain" in the entire Lake Constance region. Climbing to the top is possible, but there is an easier way. From Schwägalp (4,428 ft) in the Appenzell region, the Säntis funicular takes visitors up in spacious cabins to just below the peak. On a clear day, the view is simply breathtaking, ranging from the mostly snow-covered Alpine range down to Lake Constance and far beyond to the Black Forest and the Vosges mountains. A well-prepared footpath leads up to the cross on the mountain peak at all times of the year. Extensive visitors platforms and restaurants invite people to stay and enjoy the view.

„Settlements" on Mount Säntis date back as far as 100 years. The first mountain inn was built in 1846; a weather station followed in 1882, and in 1935, the inauguration of the funicular provided public access. Since 1956, Mount Säntis has had an additional function besides the weather station: the Swiss PTT (Post & Telecom) chose the mountain as the site for their new directional transmitter, equipped with the latest state-of-the-art telecommunication facilities. Today, Mount Säntis is one of the most important pillars in Swiss telecommunications serving 30000 telelphone subscribers, three national TV channels, three VHF radio stations and the basic network for the distribution of foreign radio and TV programmes in Switzerland.

Despite the easy access by funicular, Mount Säntis and the entire Alpstein region offers a host of opportunities for skiing and hiking, with an extensive network of clearly marked scenic tracks leading through untouched nature to various vantage points.

The Seerhein near Gottlieben (below), and „Drachenburg" Castle

Gottlieben ● ● ● ● ● ● ● ● ●

Gottlieben is the smallest independent community in Switzerland with only 300 inhabitants. The quaint former fishing village is situated on the Rhine opposite the Wollmatinger Ried nature reserve (European diploma) and boasts one of the most beautiful village squares in Switzerland with numerous Tudor-style buildings. The lakeside castle with its two interesting towers is rich in history: built between the 13th and 14th century, it used to be the residence of the Constance bishops until the late 15th century. During the Council of Constance, the Czech reformer Johannes Hus was imprisoned here until his execution, and Pope John XXIII, who was dismissed by the Council of Constance, was also held in custody in this castle. Between 1837 and 1842, the castle was owned by Prince Louis Napoleon, later Napoleon III. It has been private property since 1798.

Gottlieben is a purely pedestrian village and a mecca for gourmets with several famous restaurants. It is the ideal starting point for excursions. The Lower Lake and Rhine shipping company's liners stop in Gottlieben and transport passengers as far as Schaffhausen on a stretch of waterway that is, no doubt, one of the most beautiful in Europe. A little further up, the Rhine widens to form the Lower Lake, with many picturesque fishing villages on the Swiss shore. One of the most beautiful places is Ermatingen, also known for its „Groppenfasnacht" carnival which allegedly is the last of all annual carnivals in the world three weeks before Easter. It is celebrated with splendid processions every three years. A hiking tour along the Seerücken mountain range with its splendid view over the Lower Lake and the Rhine is much appreciated by insiders. Like a string of pearls, a number of castles, palaces and quaint old churches are special highlights on such a hiking tour.

Not only is the Swiss shore a paradise for cyclists, but also the region further inland, with an excellent 1000-mile network of cycling tracks in the canton of Thurgau. Visitors who appreciate rural life encounter numerous farms offering an insight in the authentic farming life and, in some cases, reasonable accommodation „in the barn".

Source of illustrations

Arndt 62, 63; Pfänderbahn AG 64, 65, 66, 67o., 67u.l, 67u.r.; Bucher 6, 10u., 33o.; Finke 40o., 40u.; Foto-archiv Blumeninsel Mainau 14o., 14u., 15; Kippenberg, 33u., 39u., 45o., 46o., 46u., 47, 49, 53o., 53u., 58o.l., 68/69, 71o., 71u.; Kuhnle 8/9, 12/13, 17, 18, 19, 20, 21o., 21u., 24, 25o., 25u., 26, 32, 35, 38, 39o., 41, 51o., 52, 55o., 56/57; Kur- und Verkehrsverwaltung Meersburg 43o.; Luftseilbahn Schwägalp-Säntis 72o., 72u., 73, 74; Marktanner 36o.; Napoleon Museum Arenenberg 27; Puttkammer 16o., 45u., 54o., 54u., 58o.r., 60/61, 80; Stuhler 59; Tourist-Information Konstanz 2/3, 5, 7o., 7u.; Wolff-Seybold 1, 4, 10o., 11o., 11u., 13o., 13u., 16u., 22o., 22u., 23, 28, 29o., 29u., 30, 31, 34, 36u., 37, 42, 43u., 44, 50, 51u., 55u., 58u., 70, 75, 76, 77o., 77u., 78o., 78u., cover Kuhnle.

Texts: Regine Klett und Gerhard Herr
Translation: Jutta Horton

Verlag und Vertrieb:
Stadler Verlagsgesellschaft mbH
D-78467 Konstanz, Max-Stromeyer-Straße 172

© Copyright by:
Verlag Friedr. Stadler, Konstanz
Inh. Michael Stadler

ISBN 3-7977-0416-X